ManifestNOW

A Process for Identifying and Reversing Limiting Beliefs

by D/C Russ

Author's Note

I write because it's my passion. It's one of many passions in my life. Yet, regardless of the medium, my main goal is always to provide value...to help people.

Every day I remind myself that none of this would have been possible without three key players in my life:

- My wife, Carla, for her endless support and encouragement for me to live my dreams.

- My daughter, Alexis, whose existence in this world makes me a far better man.

- And God, who has picked my sorry ass up off the ground so many times...

Thanks, to all of the characters I met along the journey who have given me more hope and inspiration than I could have ever imagined.

Now it's my turn to give back to the world all the wonderful things it has given to me.

Please visit my website, align-mentality.com to receive daily inspiration as well as a free gift: the **Ascension Cheat Sheet**. It's a 1-page guide that will encourage you to keep moving forward. It serves as a daily reminder of your true potential. Check it out, it's pretty cool.

More Books by D/C

At this point, I've decided to no longer list my other books here. For a full listing of all the incredible, life-changing books I've written, please visit my online bookshelf at:

http://align-mentality.com/bookshelf/

Thanks a lot,

D/C

Table of Contents

Preface, 6

Welcome To The Wild Ride, 12

I Have What I Want, 16

You Aren't Who You Say You Are, 18

Understanding Your Limiting Beliefs, 21

An Exercise For Identifying Limiting Beliefs, 27

Reversing A Limiting Belief, 32

Conclusion, 60

Bonus Power-Ups, 65

Closing Remarks, 68

Preface

Hey there, nice to see you! Thanks for checking out my book.

To kick this party off right, I'd like to tell you a quick story that illustrates the power that limiting beliefs can have over our lives.

Once upon a time, when I was just 6 years old, my well-meaning Kindergarten teacher told me something that would forever change the course of my life.

And although her intentions were good, her advice wasn't.

She said humbly that I wasn't a creative person. She told me that I need to stick to math and science because that's where my greatest aptitude was.

And like any typical young boy with an eager and impressionable mind, I listened to my teacher.

The advice made sense. After all, I should do what I'm best at right? And obviously the teacher knows what's best.

Why?

Well because she's a teacher of course!

My vulnerable mind was too suggestible to see the circular logic.

So without further questioning, I accepted her advice...

But a piece of me died that day. An ember in my young heart was nearly extinguished.

Years later, I continued to heed the word of this teacher by signing up for the most challenging math courses my schools offered.

I boasted proudly to my parents that one day I was going to be a rocket scientist! I even dressed up like one for career day—pocket protector and all.

My dad—a trucker—and my mom—a janitor—were so proud of me. Not because I was going to be a scientist...

But because I was following my passion in life.

Little did I know I was way off track. So needless to say, I continued to rise in the left-brain ranks.

My high school sent all the brightest freshman math students into Algebra 1 Honors.

So, naturally, I signed up for Algebra 2: a choice that later resulted in great disappointment.

You see, students were awarded a significant bonus to their GPA by being in an honors class. But I didn't get that bonus, because technically I was only in the regular Algebra 2. This was the first major blow to my confidence. And the second one came soon after.

There I was, an underdeveloped runt in a classroom of big sophomores. I stuck out like a sore thumb. They made fun of me for being small. They made fun of me for being an overachiever. They even made fun of me for being smart.

That's when things started to turn around in my life. I began to realize that I was running my head against the wall trying to be where I wasn't supposed to be.

Because, to be honest with you, I was decent at math. But I wasn't *good*.

And I knew it!

I just didn't want to let my parents down who thought I was a math whiz. But the truth is that I had to fight to bring home that 'B+' on my report card.

When I looked around at the students who were *actually* good at math, it caused me great disappointment. I felt inferior.

I really thought I was living my passion, doing what I did best. Yet, the results just weren't there.

Despite what my family told me, I knew the real truth: math was not my forte. And science made me fall asleep.

Something was wrong.

Years went by where I pretended to be someone I was not.

I was a good boy. I listened. I obeyed. I believed, deep down, that grown-ups knew what was better for me than my own heart. I let the world stick a finger in my face and tell me who I was and what to do with my life.

This limiting belief cost me years and years of failing to develop my natural-born gift of creation. I carried this belief around through college, even despite a severe phase in rebelliousness.

I even got my first job in a global investment firm, making killer money.

Yet everyday when I went to work it was like I was being shackled to my cubicle. I hated what I did so much that I fought to find micro-bursts of entertaining facets of my job. Even after nine hours sleep, I would sometimes catch myself dozing off at the computer.

When I told my family that I wanted to quit, they told me how young and immature I was. They told me to discard my youthful idealism by pounding into me "facts" about how the "real world" works.

"How the hell am I going to do this for another 40 years!?" I thought.

And moreover, why wasn't I happy? My mom had always told me that I just needed to learn to accept and be happy with where I was. And she was right to a degree.

But you wanna know one of the greatest lessons I've ever learned in life?

While it's *possible* for anyone to be happy in any situation, your unhappiness is God's message to you that something is wrong.

If you're not happy with where you are—and you *can* change it—then you've *got* to change it. If everyone kept accepting blow after blow with a fake grin plastered on their faces, the injustices of the world would never be righted.

If you're not where you want to be, then change it.

Let me tell you something else about being human. You have the God-given right to live a happy, healthy, and harmonious life filled with all the riches you desire.

The only reason you don't have the life you want is because you're harboring a false, unconscious belief system. This is the belief system fueled by the ego...the world.

And if you've noticed, the world's pretty messed up right now. So why would you listen to a single thing it has to say?

No man, no god, no guru will ever know better than your own heart does. The problem is that, as children, we're virtually defenseless against the world's poisonous belief system.

But the past is not locked in. It's not set in stone. You can access it with your mind.

And by writing this book, I intend on helping you to do just that.

If I knew about limiting beliefs when I was six, I'd have known that it was my teacher, <u>not me</u>, who wasn't creative.

Because, as they say, "if you spot it, you've got it." That's slang for "we see in others what is within ourselves".

If my teacher had thought herself to be creative, she would have found the creativity within me. Her mind would have been flexible enough to perceive my actions as creative.

Truthfully, we're all creative beings. And if you're not living that potential, then you're basically strangling your own happiness.

Creativity is the essence, the very life force, that keeps the entire Universe in motion. Everything is a part of creation and creation is in everything.

So if you're carrying around limiting beliefs from your childhood—and you most certainly are—then I invite you to dive head-first into this book, so that YOU can finally start *creating* the life that you want.

Welcome To The Wild Ride

I recognize that this book might be a bit controversial and cause some dissent among my reader base. But that's the price I'm willing to pay.

Because, as always, I am committed to getting down to the bare grit of truth so that I can deliver it to you all in a way that's straightforward and non-biased.

Obviously, of course, everything is biased in one way or the other and the only real way you can derive truth is through <u>your own</u> faculties as an infinitely knowing being. Follow what resonates with you, discard the rest.

Remember that you have all the truth inside of YOU.

In fact, everything exists *within* you because it is you who has created this entire experience for yourself.

Yes, that's right. There is no reality without your participation. You're but a physical body with senses that imperfectly perceive—a being with biases that judge everything in the world as either good or bad.

I told you this was going to be a bit crazy...

"Who is this guy anyway," you might be asking yourself.

And to that I say, "You've pretty much already hit the nail on the head."

I'm just a guy.

Just a regular person.

And that's who you are too...

The truths I'm about to share with you actually didn't come from me. They came from a source far more powerful that all of us are capable of tapping into.

I stumbled upon a discourse that I believe is going to forever change the face of how human beings begin to understand reality creation.

And, as I type these very words, I feel a strange sense of guidance luring me into writing each and every word. I was awoken abruptly by a peculiar sense of urgency, and so here I sit at 2:30am, writing this nothing-less-than-unconventional document that I'm prepared to label "self-help".

Because it is. It's *help* that you're going to do your*self*. All I'm going do is lay down a framework of understanding, to expose you to a new way of thinking about existence and the meaning of life.

I'm here to provide what they call *resonance*. Meaning, it doesn't really matter who I am -- if the contents of this book give you a certain feeling, which they very likely will, then I have reawakened in you, information that you already knew to be true.

It's your job to decode and apply that information as you see fit. And by "see" I mean "feel".

Your feelings guide you from moment to moment. It's up to you to listen to them.

Each moment you have a new bundle of countless ways that you can respond. Each moment is, in itself, filled with a virtually endless variety of opportunities that you are free to either affirm or deny. That is your free will.

Think about that: each moment...

That means NOW.

And now.

And now.

And now...

Do you get the picture? Each moment! It will really make your head spin if you think about it too much. Consider all the moments that have already passed you by. Think of all the wasted opportunities you've let slip into the past.

But before you get too hard on yourself, I want to inform you that God is laughing heartily and approvingly because you were created in His image. You were designed perfect—even in your imperfection.

He knew you would misuse and misunderstand time, and he fully Loves you for it; a Love so strong that we are literally incapable of grasping it as human beings. A Love so Powerful and Unconditional that we so often question if it's actually real.

Yes. It's real.

And this Love always will be and always has been. In fact, it's more accurately your True Identity than all of the cells in your entire body.

This is a body. This is an experience.

It is meant to be joyful. It is meant to be exciting. It is meant to be fun.

So capitalize on every moment by asking yourself, "how can I, in this very instant, follow my bliss the best way I know how?" Ask that question whenever you think of it. But don't stress out that you're not using every single moment as well as you could be.

Because that, my friend, is utterly impossible. All you need to do is make small, teeny-tiny little progress every day. And, if you do, you will wake up years, weeks, or months later and marvel in the light of your progress and accomplishments.

The goal here is not to try and be perfect. Because A) it will never happen, and B) you already are.

Such is the paradox of life!

Please, please...if you value your current mindset, do not read this book. 'Cuz it's about to turn everything you know on its head.

Consider that your disclaimer.

I Have What I Want

Like I've already mentioned, I'm just a regular guy.

But I'm a regular guy who has what he wants.

I have an amazing family and a phenomenal relationship with my wife, who avidly encourages me to live my dreams.

I have the freedom and flexibility to ask her, "Hey honey, where would you like to live next?"

We can fit everything we own into our beloved 1980 Mercedes 300SD and a small trailer. We aren't bogged down by a lot of stuff we don't need.

In fact, we regularly purge our belongings to ensure that we're keeping only the most useful and cherished items.

When we need furniture for our new home, we go on Craigslist and get it for free and fix it up, sand it, paint it, and call it our own. When we're ready to move again, we put it back on Craigslist for free.

We both decided one day that we didn't want our futon anymore. So we tore it apart and turned it into a bed that we mounted on the wall. It was awesome. And since it was so well-built and attractive, the next person to move into the house used it as a storage shelf for all of his things.

We don't sign up for credit cards or lease agreements. Nor do we have a lofty mortgage above our heads. We're free to come and go as we please by packing up our stuff and simply driving away.

Everywhere we go we get to make things better. And we can pretty much live anywhere we want, as long as there's an internet connection so that I can operate my business.

Through my business, I get to reach out and inspire thousands of people. I've even coached many people, helping them to understand and make changes with their deepest conflicts in life, which is extremely rewarding.

I don't go to a job everyday; in fact, I haven't stepped foot in any kind of physical workplace in years.

I sleep and wake up when I want. I eat amazing all-natural, chemical-free food. I love every single material item I own, and I only own things that I truly and deeply appreciate.

I have a fiery passion for the work that I do and I get to spend my time developing solid passive income streams that enable me to be financially free.

I live all of my days doing what I love: appreciating my wife, playing with my little baby girl, and following my excitement around to various deeply-fulfilling skills and passions.

Every decision in my life revolves around one core priority: true freedom. And I'm happy to report that it's actually working: I'm really grateful for everything in my life.

Why am I telling you this? To brag?

No.

I'm telling you this because it really is true what they say. You can make your dreams come true and live the life you want, if you stay focused, committed, and patient.

You see, all of this is still relatively fresh to me. It feels like just yesterday when I was pulling my hair out over the stress of not being able to pay rent.

It's a terrible feeling and I wouldn't wish it on anyone.

Furthermore, I didn't achieve all of this by following the nonsense advice of "just set the intention and visualize happy thoughts". For those of you who've consumed other Law of Attraction materials: it was not like ordering a pizza…not even close.

But there's another, far more important reason that I'm telling you all of this…

Because even when I had none of the above-mentioned things, I *still had what I wanted*.

Wait, stay with me here…

To understand what I just said, let's take a quick look at Freud's "iceberg theory" of the human mind.

You Aren't Who You Say You Are

Even before I had an amazing, loving family...

Before I had passive income...

Before I had the freedom to do what I want, when I wanted...

I STILL HAD EVERYTHING I WANTED.

And so do you. You, too, have everything you want *right now*.

I'm sure you're wondering how this can be true. "Oh no he's gonna say how I'm already some divine being and that this is just a physical experience...yada yada yada."

No, what I'm about to tell you is real, practical (and scientific) stuff.

Taking a look at Freud's 3-tiered iceberg, you have your conscious, preconscious, and unconscious minds.

For now, let's divide the iceberg into conscious—everything above surface—and subconscious—everything below the surface.

Assuming you know how an iceberg works, the part that's poking out above the water is only about 10% of the mass of the iceberg. The rest of it looms ominously, deep beneath the surface of the water.

The same is true when it comes to your mind. The part you are aware of—your conscious mind—is only a tiny portion of who you really are.

Yet, when confronted, most people staunchly defend that they are their thoughts, perceptions, and actions.

You aren't who you say you are.

Frankly, you're the whole iceberg and more. But if you had to choose, it's more accurate to claim that you're the submerged portion, rather than the visible portion.

Because it's the subconscious mind that ultimately drives your behavior, defines your emotional experience, and literally creates the reality you see in front of you.

Let me give you a powerful example of this concept working in real life:

Anthony, a colleague of mine, has written a phenomenal book that clears up many misconceptions regarding the Law of Attraction. He has appropriately named the concept [The Law of Realization](http://amazon.com/dp/b00fiv1xdo).

In this book he cites the example of a woman he once spoke with during one of his coaching sessions. This woman said she wanted to marry a wonderful man and raise children in a nice house.

This woman was a prostitute at the time.

Now I'm not judging at all. I simply want to point out an example of how our conscious wants in life mean little-to-nothing if we don't also consider our subconscious programming beneath the surface.

Come to find out, this woman did not believe, at a very deep level, that she was worthy of having what she wanted in life. Because of this, her actions were intentionally designed to ensure that she satisfied that belief. Being a prostitute is a great way to make sure no family-minded man will ever want to marry you.

So, as Anthony states in his book, this woman's beliefs fueled her actions and her actions then fueled her beliefs. When she looked around at her life, it was abundantly clear that she indeed was not worthy of having the life that she wanted.

Around and around we go...where we stop nobody knows.

You see, a misunderstanding of whom you really are leads to a vicious cycle that keeps you firmly stuck in life no matter how much you *want* something to be true.

To change your life, you have to change your beliefs.

Because based on your beliefs, it is quite easily arguable that you do, in fact, have everything you want in life right now...

...maybe not at a conscious level...

...but deep down, your subconscious mind is churning out the reality that you programmed into it.

And so I urge you: when it comes to creating the life that you want, pay very close attention to what's deep beneath the surface.

Understanding Your Limiting Beliefs

Fortunately, you can utilize your conscious mind to make changes to your underlying belief system.

But first, you need to learn how to spot your limiting beliefs. In this chapter, I will show you some examples of limiting beliefs so you can begin to identify them in your own life.

It's important to understand that your limiting beliefs are already manifesting themselves in your life. Your beliefs lie deep in the subconscious mind, which as we've learned, is the powerhouse for reality creation.

In this sense, you are always manifesting, whether you like it or not. It is important to first understand this fact before you go off trying to attract something you desire.

To be blunt, you can desire something all you want, you can visualize 17 times daily, and you can recite a thousand mantras...

...but if your deep-seated beliefs aren't in agreement with your conscious desires, guess what? You can keep dreamin' buddy.

So let's learn how to really cut to the core and rebuild the foundation before we start adding more stories to the house.

Step one in creating your reality is to first *realize* how you've gotten to be where you currently are. This entails being self-aware of your thoughts, emotions, and actions.

As you practice this process, you'll begin to notice how you sabotage yourself through self-talk: "Yeah I'd like to have that but it's just way too hard..." Or, "Yeah, but it'll never work." Or even, "The truth is, you have to [have a lot of education OR be very attractive OR have money OR know people OR be really lucky]."

You'll also find that you do things, usually unknowingly, that serve as confirmations to your limiting beliefs. For example you may get ready to start a project but you decide to plan profusely instead of just starting. You'll overwhelm yourself with all the things you have to do and then give up.

Or another common road block people get themselves into is called paralysis by analysis. There's a tendency for people to want to know everything before taking the first step. They want to make sure everything is perfect first. In reality, this is impossible because nothing will ever be perfect. There are potentially dozens of limiting beliefs associated with these tendencies: "I'm not good enough", "People won't take me seriously unless I'm perfect", or "I can't actually do this so I'm going to keep myself busy in order to pretend like I'm doing it". Keep in mind that this is largely subconscious and you might not see it until you resolve to look for it.

Also note that a limiting belief is usually characterized by a strong negative emotion. The emotion is trying to reveal your limiting beliefs to you. So listen up!

If you find yourself getting sad, angry, or afraid, then it usually means you're doing or thinking something that's counter-productive to your happiness. Your limiting beliefs are writing the script of your life, usually beneath your stream of conscious awareness.

The process of identifying limiting beliefs takes great introspection and self-awareness, which is where your conscious mind steps in as a valuable tool. You've got to want to change.

You must become a detective commissioned to investigate the depths of your subconscious mind.

The way you do this is by simply taking a look around. Look at your life. Literally. Look around. What do you have? Take a few moments to notice what you have and what you're thankful for.

Now, what do you <u>not have</u>? This part might not be as fun. But it's crucial to shine the light into the darkness if you ever want to dissolve it.

Think about your desires and then take a few moments to see which of your desires you don't have. Pick one. We'll take it slow and just work with one thing at a time here.

Let's say you don't have the financial abundance you desire.

It's easy to then say "OK I don't have the financial abundance that I desire, so I must not believe that I deserve the financial abundance I desire."

But it's far more complex than that, and you're going to have to dig a little deeper. You didn't think this was going to be *easy*, did you?

The truth is, you could have ten—or even 100—limiting beliefs that are preventing you from financial abundance. Once you start chipping away at these beliefs, you will immediately begin to attract more financial abundance (provided that you are taking <u>Aligned Action</u> to do so). For more on aligned action, see my previous book: http://amazon.com/dp/b00ewok94m

Action is a crucial step in this process. By physically moving toward your goals, your limiting beliefs will inevitably surface and be much easier to spot. You can't help but to run into them when you're physically approaching whatever it is that you want. Just one small step per day is all you really need.

But I digress...

The way you know if a limiting belief is standing between you and your goal is by introspecting and listening to your feelings.

I'm going to give you some examples of beliefs that I personally struggled with when it came to financial abundance. But first, here's a really quick strategy you can use to make the connection between your belief and how it may be limiting your abundance:

Simply take a moment to visualize the belief in question (or the behavior that stems from it), and ask yourself: is this something that a magnificently wealthy person would do? Or can I see a poor person doing/believing this?

Obviously, if your desires aren't financial, substitute "magnificently wealthy person" with whatever it is you desire, i.e. "person with an amazing relationship".

So here's a brief and incomplete list of my own personal limiting beliefs that I had to overcome to experience success. A few of these might surprise you—sometimes a belief that seems completely unrelated to financial success actually can hinder it.

- Hard work is the key to success. For this reason I must work all day as much as I can, squeezing out every last minute possible.
- The world doesn't give a damn about me, I'm all alone and I have to do this all by myself. So screw 'em.
- Money is hard to come by. Once you get it, you've got to hang on to it with a kung-fu death grip.

- It's important to always give more than you receive. If someone asks you for a favor, you should always do it for free because it's the nice thing to do.
- No one wants to listen to me. What do I know, I'm just a kid.
- You're a nobody until you have money.
- You've got to do a lot of things you don't want to do if you ever expect to make money.
- People piss me off. They're lazy and they never follow through.
- The government sucks at managing resources.
- I'm better than everyone else.

So, as you can see, there are a lot of them. I could probably come up with at least 30 different beliefs that I personally held which were preventing me from financial abundance.

I want to make it clear that these are only beliefs, not facts. Furthermore, whether I knew it or not, I always maintained the ability to choose which ones I wanted to keep and which ones were no longer serving me. That's the power of your free will, your conscious mind.

The thing is, some of your beliefs might even be true to a certain degree. For example, the government *does* suck at managing resources. That's not exactly an unreasonable belief. But it's the **energy *behind that belief*** that's really disrupting your flow. You've got to accept it and let it go.

There's a difference between saying something as-a-matter-of-fact, and then saying it with negative energy behind it. Frankly, I hesitated to put this in because so many people will use it as a weapon against themselves: "Whaaaatttt...I'm just saying...I don't *mean* anything by it, I'm just being honest..."

Bullshit. Your subconscious mind sees right through that bullshit so don't pretend it can't. Refrain from using your words and actions to conceal your deep-seated beliefs. You cannot trick your subconscious mind and you certainly can't fool the Universe.

The discrepancy between your actions and the underlying energy is best illustrated by the Training Balance Scale. This is an extremely important concept that is applicable in nearly every situation. I addressed the Training Balance Scale in my previous book. You can read more about it here:

http://amazon.com/dp/b00ewok94m

So this leads into the question: how can <u>you</u> spot your own limiting beliefs? Well, your limiting beliefs are almost always characterized by negative emotions. These emotions result from the fact that you're doing or thinking something unproductive or harmful.

Let's take an example:

An Exercise For Identifying Limiting Beliefs

First, name something that you want.

It could be anything: financial security, freedom to travel, explosively orgasmic sex, a wonderful family, loyal friends, a freelance career, ability to pursue an expensive hobby or a passion, etc.

So tell me, why don't you have it? Why have you been unable to achieve that desire?

Go on. Say it. Either to yourself or aloud.

Stop and answer the question.

Now ask yourself: "What's preventing me from having what I want?"

Be completely honest.

If you need to get a pen and paper, go for it. Come up with a quick list of reasons why you can't have what you want. These are your limiting beliefs. You can tell they're your limiting beliefs because they make you feel bad: heavy, depressed, stressed, etc.

Now allow yourself to come to the full realization that you do not have your desire.

Take a moment to see your magnificent desire devolving into your present reality. If your desire is to have a loving relationship with your spouse, visualize all the pain and tension involved between you and your significant other.

If your desire is to be your own boss, visualize all the anger, frustration, and resentment you have against your current boss.

Whatever your desire is, focus now on the fact that you do not have it.

How does it make you feel?

Think of all the past instances that solidify your painful reality. Allow all the bad feelings to surface. Remember that the feelings themselves <u>cannot</u> hurt you, only your reaction to them can cause harm.

Fully engage with not having your desire. You may feel a strong emotional reaction at this point. The stronger the emotional reaction, the more limiting that the underlying beliefs are.

Really sink into this painful reality and allow it to consume you. Remember that you're safe.

If you find you're experiencing a really intense negative reaction, it usually means you've been letting this limiting belief persist for far too long. And <u>now</u> is always the right time to deal with it. Not tomorrow, not "someday"...*now*.

Become your own observer. Pay close attention to how you feel as if you are a scientist conducting observational research for your experiment.

Take note of where in your body you feel any pain, discomfort, emptiness, tension, heaviness, stress, etc. Do a head-to-toe scan of your body. Where is the sensation? Your head? Stomach? Throat? Jaw? All over?

Describe the sensation. Imagine it had physical characteristics. What color is it? Does it have any motion? How large is it? Is it a band, a disc, a ball...? What material is it made of? Be as detailed as possible in your description of the feeling. Spend a minute or two becoming very familiar with the sensation you're experiencing.

Think back in your past to other times when you've felt this. Try to go as far back as you can. What was happening? Who was there?

This marks the initial or early formation of this limiting belief. This is when you first began to tell yourself that it's true.

Keep going through these motions until you feel sufficiently in-touch with the belief and its origins.

From here, I have a couple routes you can take. You can relax, accept, and breathe through any emotions you might be experiencing. Or, if you're in a safe, comfortable space I invite you to dig deeper using The Haymaker Method in the next chapter.

But in case you aren't at liberty to express yourself aloud if need be, let me first walk you through the closing of the identifying portion of this exercise:

So I want you to just breathe deeply and relax. Be joyful. You're connecting with yourself. Accept your emotions. Allow them. Watch them rise to the surface of your experience and be grateful for the sensation.

By curiously observing and peacefully allowing your feelings, you're actually in the process of releasing them. This helps to take a huge load off the task of reprogramming your limiting beliefs.

Just know that I am with you through the pain. I know what it's like. Many people do. We're all with you. You can feel us through prayer. You can hear us in music. People everywhere are waking up to the various energies—good and "bad"—of the human experience.

Keep breathing. Feel yourself relax and sink into the feeling. Just for a moment, enjoy being human. Celebrate your ability to feel.

Sometimes people are ashamed of their feelings. We live in a world where it's not socially acceptable to express your hardship and difficulties. But it is YOUR courage that will guide this planet into a new realm of existence. It is YOUR strength to be open and vulnerable that will make the difference.

So again, I invite you to be grateful for your pain. I invite you to welcome your limiting beliefs proudly, as if you're exploring a magnificent cave and observing its geological features.

Be human. Be aware. Be curious. Be open.

As you continue to breathe, relax your body. Repeat this phrase aloud or to yourself: *"Even though I believe 'X', I fully and deeply accept myself."* Say it as few or as many times as you'd like.

Remember that strength lies in vulnerability. Control lies in your ability to give it up.

For now, just feel...

...just <u>be</u>.

Reversing A Limiting Belief

Okay now it's time to delve a bit deeper into your belief and into the process of reversing it. The following processes have been used thousands of times in various ways by healers all across the planet and throughout time. The basic structure is quite simple, but you may find some of the exercises to be particularly intense or difficult.

I've learned these methods through my time spent with and among healers, through vigorous study, and through personal experimentation and innovation.

The best way to conduct a healing session, either on yourself or someone else, is simply to be present and respond to whatever happens to come up in the moment.

It is for this reason that any person is capable of self-healing and healing others. You are but a conduit for the endlessly abundant Love energy that surrounds us everywhere.

And if you think that's "too hippy"…

…then get a grip.

Lots of people who need healing in their lives refuse to connect with the process because it makes them uncomfortable or because they feel ashamed.

Trust me, I know what it's like because I've been there **many** times.

But what it always came down to for me is a simple choice: would I rather be stuck with limiting beliefs and repressed emotions or am I okay with being a little uncomfortable so I can live my dreams and achieve higher levels of creational free will?

The choice is simple. And I've found that, generally speaking, the further out of your comfort zone you can go, the more growth and learning that results.

So I wanted this discussion to be a precursor into this next section because some of the things I mention/suggest may make you tremendously uncomfortable. You may not have ever heard of or done anything close to this.

It's for this reason that I strongly urge you to do the more intense healing exercises alone, when you have the liberty to say, do, or look any way you want/need to.

I realize that it's difficult for most people to have a significant block of time alone without being disturbed. Just do the best you can.

Ideally, you'll want to get in a place where, if needed, you can make loud noises without disturbing anyone. Sometimes it helps to put on loud music to help drown out and distort sounds.

Some of these exercises can be done in passing, while others are best suited for a quiet, more private environment.

I use a boxing analogy to distinguish between the two: the "Jab Methods" are quick and simple, and they can be done almost anywhere. "The Haymaker Method" is way more complex and in-depth and will require you to carve out time and space.

Generally speaking, the jab methods can be done several times per day, while the haymaker method is capable of producing *enormous* change in just one session.

You're welcome to do any of these exercises with, or in the presence of, someone you deeply trust who is mature and understands your goals of healing. If you know someone like this, you must cherish him or her. It takes a special person to be willing to engage in the methods I am about to describe.

I will now offer you a series of things for you to try when the time is right. Only you really know when the time is right. I think the best time to try these methods is when you're actually experiencing the limiting belief. This is usually characterized by negative emotion, heaviness, depression, sadness, or any type of low feeling.

However, sometimes the best way to defeat a limiting belief is to throw jabs at it throughout the day. These strategies do not require you to actually be immersed in the emotion, which is why the jab methods may be more convenient than the haymaker approach. For those of you not familiar with a haymaker, it's a term used in boxing to describe a heavy and extremely powerful punch intended to knock out an opponent in a single blow.

Each strategy has its strengths and weaknesses. For example, a haymaker usually requires a tremendous amount of energy and can leave the boxer defenseless for a time, whereas a jab is quick and the boxer can maintain a defensive posture. When a haymaker lands, it can be devastating...but it must be timed correctly, otherwise it's a huge wasted investment of energy.

In the case of removing a limiting belief, you should incorporate a mixture of both strategies. Whenever you can, take some quick shots at dismantling your limiting belief by just being aware when it surfaces, and then correcting it.

Think of it like walking a dog. And I'll cite The Dog Whisperer here: when Cesar Millan is training a dog, he makes tiny but frequent micro adjustments with the leash proactively, *before* the dog (or in this case, the limiting belief) gets out of hand. The dog has a short attention span and must be constantly reminded of how he should behave until it becomes second nature.

You can throw jabs all day, making tiny adjustments whether you're at work, in your car, or surfing the web.

Sometimes, though, a more intense approach is necessary to really break through your mental barriers and clear yourself out emotionally.

Although science has yet to prove it, it's pretty well accepted among healers, yoga masters, and body workers that emotions are physically stored in the human body. Repeated thoughts that disempower you (aka limiting beliefs) and make you feel bad will actually store themselves in your body. In order to release them, you may have to pull a 'haymaker' approach.

The advantage of this approach is that it's tremendously clearing and can be an extremely effective way to blast out all of that accumulated, "stuck" emotional energy.

The disadvantage is that it requires a greater investment of energy and emotional resources. This approach demands more time and space in order to truly give it justice. The haymaker strategy can take anywhere from about 20 minutes to several hours.

As you read on and begin to try the jab methods, you may increasingly feel a need to pursue the more thorough route using the haymaker strategy. In this book, I will discuss this approach, but honestly if you can afford it, I strongly recommend going to see a trained healer who specializes in emotional release and reversing limiting beliefs. Not only do they have lots of practice and experience, but they will also usually have a suitable environment for a heavy duty healing experience.

So without further adieu...

Jab Method #1 - Straight Talk

Think about a desire you have. It's helpful to say it aloud if you're at liberty to do so. Otherwise you can just do the exercise in your head: e.g. "I desire ___." or "I want to ___."

Now answer the following question as quickly as you can, paying special attention to the first thing that pops into your head. Don't be afraid to admit to yourself whatever comes up.

The question is:

"Why don't you have your desire?"

Now take that response and construct a statement with it: e.g. "I do not have a fulfilling, committed relationship because I'm not attractive enough."

Or, "I am not making as much passive income as I'd like because I need to write more books."

Or, "I could never be an entrepreneur because I don't have any skills or original ideas."

Once you've constructed your statement, then just ask yourself very simply and directly:

Do I want this belief?

If your answer is 'Yes' then you need not go any further. It may be that, for whatever reason, you're okay with writing more books or doing what it takes to make yourself more attractive. Maybe you see it as motivation to accomplish these goals in life. And that's totally fine. No one's saying you have to change your beliefs.

However, if your answer is 'No' then it's time to take a few jabs at the belief. And as an author who enjoys book sales, I wish I could give you the magical formula for doing so.

But I promised I'd keep it real and not BS you. So, instead, I'll encourage you to figure it out by giving you a few examples. The main goal is to determine what **feels** best. I cannot stress that enough. Moreover, what feels good this time might feel fake or forced the next time you go to take a jab at your belief. In that case, just switch up your jab. Throw a right, then a left, then a right. Stick and move, comrade, stick and move.

You could go a number of routes with this one. If you subscribe to the transient nature of the present moment and the illusory nature of time, you might try the good old "I do have [insert desire], I'm just waiting patiently for it to manifest physically."

Or you could try something more practical: "I don't yet have [desire] because I believe ___. However I recognize that this is only a belief and that it's not necessarily true."

How about, "I can be an entrepreneur if I want to. Everyone has original ideas, even me. I just need to 1) understand what skills I DO have, and 2) learn whatever skills I think I will need."

Sometimes what I do when I hear a limiting belief chattering in my mind is basically tell it to shut up. I call this voice the devil.

He'll try to jab me but I'll dodge it, only to punch back by saying, "bullshit, that ain't true and you know it!" He will normally go away. But make no mistake, the devil always returns...that son of a gun...

But what I've learned recently is that the devil is actually your friend. You could easily construe him as a bad watch dog. Even though he barks a lot, once in a while he's actually barking for a good reason. "BARK, BARK...HEY YOU'VE GOT A LIMITING BELIEF HERE...BARK, BARK".

Anyway, you've just got to work with it. Find what works best for you. Maybe instead of telling the dog to shut up, you soothe him by petting him and saying, "Shhh, doggie it's okay. It's just the mailman."

God I hope this analogy is still working for you...

So, here's Jab Method #1 in a nutshell:
- "I desire ___."
- "I do not have ___ because I believe ___."
- Jab back at the belief

I encourage you to use your own wording and to switch it up whenever you feel like. The beauty of this method is that you call all the shots and you throw all the jabs. Just do what feels good. Once you get good at it, you'll know when your limiting belief is about to strike and you can jab back right away. Sometimes the best defense is a good offense.

The key with this strategy is repetition. You want to become very efficient with your jabs so that you can strike quickly, many times throughout the day. You'll probably notice a difference in just a few days. Look for feelings of empowerment, confidence, "lightness", or relief. You may even find yourself smiling more often as your limiting beliefs begin to loosen their grip on you.

Remember that there's nothing "wrong" with limiting beliefs. Don't panic and don't beat yourself up. Just be honest with yourself. Be open when it comes to admitting to yourself that you have limiting beliefs. Don't be scared, don't be angry. If you relate this to boxing again, the fighter who's confident in his training always remains calm, even after he receives a painful blow.

Keep your head in the game and always focus on how you're feeling. Whatever you gotta do, always try to feel just a little bit better.

Jab Method #2 - Eye Movement

This is based on a technique called EMDR: Eye Movement Desensitization and Reprocessing, as developed by Francine Shapiro.

The method works really well whenever your limiting beliefs suddenly attack you and your emotions are up.

If something in life suddenly triggers an emotion that's associated with your limiting belief, you may want to try Jab Method #2.

For example, maybe all of a sudden you feel sad because something reminded you that "I'm not good enough".

What you want to do is let that emotion play out. If there is an image associated with it, go ahead and visualize it.

Stay focused on that image and/or feeling. On a scale of 1-10, how intense is the feeling?

Now, notice where your eyes are. They may be fixed in a certain position. You can visualize that this is where your belief and its associated emotion got 'stuck' in your neurology.

What you want to do is randomly move your eyes around while you focus on the emotion. For a reason that is not entirely understood, this 'unsticks' the belief and its associated feelings.

Keep focused on the emotion (this will be tricky while you're rolling your eyes around in your head, but do your best) and repeat the belief to yourself while you move your eyes. If you feel the urge to sigh, this is a great sign that you're getting your circuits moving again.

Do this for however long you feel instinctively guided to do. Anywhere from about 10 seconds to 30 seconds is all you need.

Okay stop and relax. Now, on a scale of 1-10, how intense is the feeling? You may notice that the number went down slightly. Take 10-30 seconds to relax and do it again. You may do this as many times as you wish.

The reason this works is because your eyes are closely connected to your brain. Often, when you have a thought that produces an intense emotion, your eyes will react to it by sticking in a certain position. This method will help you "unstick" your eyes so that you can scramble the image and begin to dissolve the emotion associated with the belief.

You may refer to the process in the last chapter to help you really recall the limiting belief. Sometimes it's helpful to delve deep into your past to discover the earliest time you've experienced this feeling.

Once you've done that, you can hold that image or feeling in your mind and then move your eyes around. The stronger the feeling when you do this, the better the results.

You can also intuitively move your finger in front of your face and follow it with your eyes. Again, do this while holding the feeling and/or image.

There are many therapists who use this technique for a variety of unique cases. You might consider finding one in your area. Also, I've heard of therapists and coaches being able to do this method over Skype, which is really cool.

I invite you to check out this YouTube video: http://www.youtube.com/watch?v=Dsyg2ee0yMQ. This guy explains it really well and also shares his personal experience with the method.

So, here's Jab Method #2 in a nutshell:
- Allow the feeling to come and hold onto it
- If there are images, focus on visualizing them
- Intuitively move your eyes around for 10-30 seconds
- Relax for 10-30 seconds, repeat as necessary

Jab Method #3 - Tapping

The third jab method involves a series of movements where you will tap on specific parts of your body. The way it works is by stimulating the main energy meridians on the body.

Although this type of healing has been performed for millennia, namely in the East in the form of acupressure, the specific method that I will share with you is known as the Emotional

Freedom Technique, or EFT. It's also known informally as the *tapping method*.

This method commonly incorporates power-ups such as mantras, affirmations, breathing exercises, body postures, etc. For your convenience, I've included the most effective of these power-ups at the end of this book.

You can absolutely incorporate these power-ups with any of the methods described in this book. I want you to realize that the most effective healing results from your freedom to mix and match techniques and methods in a way that feels best to you.

Okay, back to Jab Method #3.

The best time to do this method is when you're feeling pretty good, and you are simply aware of your emotional difficulty, but not totally drowned and consumed by it.

But again, if you've got some spare time and want to engage in a healing session, feel free to use the procedure in the last chapter to bring up the limiting belief and the emotion(s) behind it.

Ah...yes...healing limiting beliefs...my favorite pastime.

Kidding.

But seriously, it's quite enjoyable once you begin to see the results.

Okay, so for this method, I want you to take your index and middle fingers and curl them slightly. Now tap these two fingers repeatedly on your wrist. Do the same with the other hand.

That'll help get your blood pumping.

You want to be pretty firm in your tapping but for God's sake don't hurt yourself. I think this method works best if you're able to relax into the tapping.

With this method, there are a series of points on your body that you will tap on, in a specific sequence. We will get to this sequence in just a bit.

There are some discrepancies among various practitioners of this method that include a slightly different set of points. Also, some say to use both hands; others say using just one hand to go through the points is sufficient. Some people advocate using both hands at the same time, each hand slightly out of synch with each other.

So which of these is the best?

<u>The best way is what works best for **you**.</u> This is an extremely important concept in virtually all areas of life: healing, business, relationships, manifestation, etc.

Listen to the teachers, get people's advice and perspective, and then tailor it to suit you. That's why, in order to get these methods to work most effectively is to 1) actually do them, and 2) experiment with them.

But really quickly, I'll tell you right now that *maybe* 10% of the people who read this book will actually try even one of these methods. Just food for thought.

So for the purposes of this book, I will discuss the most popular version of the tapping method. Along the way I will indicate the differences between other versions of this method.

But in all of these variations, the main concept is the same: to stimulate energy flow throughout the body in order to facilitate movement of these energies along the major channels of the body. It's based on a principle that states that the mind, the heart, and the body are all connected and influence each other.

At each point tap anywhere from 5-7 times, or about as many times as it takes you to complete one full breath. You can synchronize your breathing with the tapping if it feels right. Trust me: you'll know if something feels right. Don't second-guess yourself.

You may also recite mantras while you run through the sequence of tapping. Mantras help to keep you focused. You'll want to stay present with this method so that you can notice any cognitive shifts that occur, like emotional easing or the emergence of sudden flashes of insight.

I think the coolest thing about EFT is the fact that you can pretty much tap on anything: fears, sadness, depression, anxiety, anger, a headache, body pain, and both bad *and* good thoughts.

Furthermore, EFT can never hurt you. It can only help you. For instance, you can tap on a positive affirmation OR a negative one! Cool huh? This means that you could be holding a thought or repeating a phrase like "I deserve financial abundance" and it will be just as effective to tap on a phrase like "I do NOT deserve financial abundance." Either way works the same. You can't lose!

Your brain and body have **enormous** healing potential. Basically all you have to do is get the energy flowing again and your body handles the rest. It's magnificent!

The only reason we get messed up in the first place is because we unwittingly allow our minds and bodies to hang on to the trauma. This is done many ways, for example when you do not express and release emotion.

There is a widespread misunderstanding of emotions in this world. People are encouraged to hide their emotions and keep them trapped inside. It's considered bad to cry, for example.

When these emotions are continuously shoved down and repressed over many years—which is often the case—they accumulate in the body, restricting energy flow and causing various problems that manifest in the form of physical disease, mental degeneration, and even financial crises and car crashes. More on all that to come in later books.

Just look at babies for example. Whenever the *slightest* thing goes wrong in a baby or a small child's life, they instantly begin crying. And they're good at it too! They can literally start crying at the drop of the hat. And most of the time they cry it out and begin to feel better immediately. They're able to stop crying just about as fast as they started. That's because the emotion gets expressed and released, rather than repressed and stored.

And this is because babies and small children have not been on the planet long enough to have been indoctrinated by social constructions that tell you what to do with your emotions. They have not yet become corrupt by the darkness that has fallen over Planet Earth. But, don't worry, soon they will. Just like you. Just like me.

It's sad, really sad. But at the same time it's beautiful. And we owe it to ourselves to see it like this. Because it's this kind of thinking that will eventually lead to our salvation and the future

Peace on Planet Earth. Soon we will all establish a new collective of standards for Earth's people, one based on Love and Acceptance, not Fear and Guilt.

...

So, back to EFT...

Let's take a look at the sequence, shall we?

- Tapping Point 1: inside corner of your eyebrow, just above your eye
- Point 2: just past the outside corner of your eye
- 3: cheekbone, just below your eye
- 4: upper lip, just below your nose
- 5: just below your bottom lip, above your chin
- 6: just below your collar bone, slightly offset
- 7: on your side in the middle of your ribcage
- 8: under your nipple between your ribs
- 9: top of your head (where a baby's soft spot is)
- 10: the side of your finger tips: turn your hand sideways with your thumb up, and tap on the side of the first finger joints on your thumb, index, middle, and pinky finger. They indicate skipping your ring finger, I don't know why, but it won't hurt anything if you tap that finger too.

This is the method that I was first taught and the one that I use most regularly. There is slight variation as to the exact location of these points but pretty much everyone agrees that you don't have to be precise. And moreover, I encourage you to **feel** each point so that you can find the place that seems most effective for you.

Don't worry if you're having trouble locating these points. Here's a great video that shows you how this method is done.
(http://www.youtube.com/watch?v=SudAHmVTARA)

I chose this video because it is short and the woman in it is an EFT coach.

Notice that points #8 and #10 are omitted, and that's totally OK. Also notice that for the last three points in her sequence, she is using not only two fingers, but ALL four fingers (no thumb). This is also perfectly acceptable.

In this video, she is using EFT to start the day and help her to have a great day. This is just one of virtually unlimited ways that you can use this technique. Notice that she's using positive affirmations. You can also tap on negative emotions, like fear: "I am worried that today is going to be awful!" Again, you cannot mess this technique up...

Unless your fingernails are too sharp and you stab yourself in the eye. Then you can use the tapping method to help with the pain.

This woman has other videos for different uses of EFT. I encourage you to check out more videos if this is something that you feel is helpful for you.

I'll say it again: please feel free to customize this routine to suit you. If you're in public, you can tap on only the more discrete points, muttering the affirmations quietly to yourself or even if your mind.

Go ahead and mix and match whatever works for you. I wish I could tell you exactly how to do it, but I'm afraid I can't. That's for you to discover.

Jab Method #4 - Fake It 'Till You Make It

This is my favorite jab method. You've got to be a real boss to pull this one off.

I'm not sure if this method is for everybody. It takes guts. It takes fire.

I really believe this method is the #1 best way to conquer a limiting belief. It requires that you stare down your limiting belief like an underdog boxer sizing up a world champ.

One way that you can fake it 'till you make is by picking a belief that you want to have and just start confirming it for yourself.

Don't pick something that's so unbelievable that it's out of your reach. Start with something that's within your grasp.

For example, if you wanted to create a belief that's more conducive to your financial abundance, you might say something like, "I have an effective relationship with money."

So you do the standard mantra recitals and pen-and-paper jot-downs, if that feels good...

But, more importantly, you start looking for evidence to support that belief. And trust me, it's there.

Let's say you want to be a good singer. But you damn well know you're not a good singer. So in order to get this method to work, you wouldn't say something like, "I'm a good singer." That's too far out of reach for now.

Instead, say something like, "I can become a better singer."

What works for me is I pick something that fires me up but that's still in reach. Then, I look myself in the mirror and say it with conviction while I'm staring myself in the eyes. Sometimes I'll mix in some EFT to really etch it into my soul. And, of course, power-ups are good here too!

Then, I just set the **firm** intention to confirm that assertion. So I end up looking for evidence that either supports my having it or supports my ability to get it.

You can also do this in reverse. Let's say you know a guy, Steve, who pisses you off. The natural tendency is to get pissed off. But let's say that you think you're a real champ and you decide to use D/C Russ' Jab Method #4.

You're going to first identify the fact that you have a limiting belief about Steve. Namely, you believe that Steve's a dick. The fact that you think he's a dick makes you angry.

When you're angry you don't make good decisions. You're wasting your time and energy being angry instead of doing something productive.

Therefore your belief is limiting you. In other words, it's a *limiting* belief.

But, again, you're a champ: you have the guts to recognize your limiting belief. And you're not afraid to admit the problem isn't with Steve, it's with YOU.

So you think to yourself: "maybe Steve pisses me off so much because I see something in him that's actually ***in me***."

Maybe Steve is your co-worker and he's disorganized. Maybe Steve is your husband and he doesn't take care of things that require his attention. Maybe Steve is your son and he procrastinates on doing his homework. Maybe Steve is your know-it-all neighbor. Or maybe Steve is a politician who's a selfish liar.

That's cool if you want to be pissed off at Steve the rest of your life. But if you're a student of D/C Russ, you're going to realize that, in some ways, *YOU* are actually Steve.

And, let me tell ya, nothing melts away a limiting belief faster than when you start to see evidence in your life that contradicts it. If you're badass enough to take a hard look at your life, you'll notice that you're somewhat disorganized too. Maybe you don't take care of business. You probably procrastinate. Or maybe you think you "know it all". And if you dig deep enough, you'll see the many ways that you can be selfish and untruthful.

Recap of Jab Method #4:
- Choose a reasonable belief you want to have and then look for evidence to support it.
- Pick a belief that you **don't** want to have and then look for evidence that contradicts it.

But wait! Hold the phone! There's a second, <u>far more powerful</u> application of Jab Method #4.

Did you know that you can fake it 'till you make it with your actions too?

I'll shed a little light by telling you a personal story about how I did this in my own life.

Once upon a time not too long ago, I had a horribly debilitating belief that I wasn't worth what I thought I was worth. For the longest time I didn't want to admit it. I kept reassuring myself that "Of course I'm worth it!" even though there was a powerful belief deep beneath the surface showing me otherwise.

This caused me to severely under-price my freelancing services. I would always go above and beyond to make my clients happy without making sure I also was happy with the arrangement. This cost me a LOT of anger and resentment and caused me a great deal of pain.

And of course, like a typical human being does, I proceeded to project this anger on my client: "He doesn't pay me enough...he's a cheap bastard...he's taking advantage of me..." So on and so forth...

The pain was so great, I finally had to sit down and level with myself: "Why does this keep happening to me? What am I doing wrong?" That's when I discovered, to my great chagrin, that *I* was the cheap bastard. And I was taking advantage *of myself*.

There were so many things that I could have done to prevent myself from being in situations where I was doing revision after revision for a client that was paying me half of what I thought I was worth on a conscious level.

But like all unlearned lessons in this Universe, it kept coming back around again to punch me in the face. But this next time I was prepared.

A client emailed me after agreeing to hire me for a web design project. He said kindly, "Hey I was just wondering what your estimate for this website is, so that I can budget accordingly."

The first thing that went through my mind is, "Hmm...well he's a nice guy, so I have to cut him a good deal."

I was afraid to charge too much because I might make him mad. So I thought about what a fair price would be and then subtracted $200 from it.

And right before I was about to click 'Send' I took a look at my measly $600 estimate. I was stunned! Here I was about to do this same damn thing...AGAIN!

So I stopped immediately and asked myself what a person *without* this limiting belief would do in this situation. I realized suddenly that I was going to have to fake it 'till I make it.

This inspired me to actually do some research. I pretended that I was a highly valued web designer, which in reality wasn't too far off. I know my stuff, and I **always** do an excellent job.

So I allowed that grain of truth to really blossom. And, because I had lots of evidence to support that belief, I used it as leverage against my limiting belief that I wasn't worth it.

After reading about website design pricing and calling a firm to get a price quote, I realized that it was quite reasonable to charge more than $600. And now I actually had evidence to back it up. Facing my limiting belief led me to actually investigate the pricing.

And the funny thing is, I didn't even have to quote him a price. I merely presented the findings from my research so that he could see the rates for himself.

I left it open to negotiation by stating the market value of the service. And even though I was willing to do it for less than what I quoted him, he simply replied back, "Yeah sounds good, $1200 is definitely within my budget. Thanks a lot!"

And that was it. Done deal.

Simply by being willing to confront my limiting belief, I literally doubled my money. It took me all of 15 minutes to do the research, and I saved myself an immense amount of pain from doing something for unfair compensation.

This is a prime example of how you can use Jab Method #4 through your actions. And I truly believe that it is the most powerful jab method for reversing a limiting belief.

All you have to do is confront the limiting belief by acting "as-if". Just ask yourself what a person without your limiting belief would do. Then just fake it 'till you make it.

The catch with this method is that you have to be tough enough to face that limiting belief head on. And you've got to finally put your foot down and do the exact opposite of what your limiting belief has you programmed to do.

This is a pretty difficult method because it requires an enormous level of introspection and an extreme resolve to change it.

You have to look for the pain in your life and have the guts to admit that it's YOU who is causing yourself that pain, no matter how external the phenomenon may seem.

Only someone who is truly committed to personal growth will be able to pull this off.

Jab Method #5 - A Little Help Here!

I debated on whether or not I should include this method. It's a method that I use often in my life and I'd say it has a powerful effect, even though some people have a hard time connecting with it.

Whenever you identify or notice a limiting belief, sometimes the best thing to do is admit defeat and turn to a higher power.

I used to get anxious (and sometimes I still do) that my dreams and goals aren't manifesting fast enough.

When this happens, I simply talk to God and say something to the effect of, "God, I'm experiencing ____, and I don't think it's helpful to me to feel this way. I offer this feeling to you, Lord, to heal and guide me."

There are lots of ways you can phrase it, just talk to God like you're talking to a friend. This method is great because it allows you to become more connected with God and Source Energy.

Of course, you may pray to any "higher" entity that you want to. I just use 'God' and 'Jesus' because that's what I'm most comfortable with.

If your emotion persists after offering it to God, then perhaps you should just allow the feeling. Experience it.

It may be that it's in your highest interest to feel how you're feeling because the emotion is trying to teach you something. In which case "getting rid of it" isn't what you need to do. Perhaps try inviting the emotion in, thanking it and casually observing it. Be still and remain calm, comrade. It will all start to make sense very soon.

In the meantime, just chill out and have a little faith, will ya?

The Haymaker Method

For this method, you're going to want to give yourself some time and space. An hour should be plenty. Note that you do not have to do this entire thing in one sitting, although it's recommended for maximum benefit.

Start by identifying the belief you want to work with. Figure out what you want, why you're eliminating the belief, what you hope to achieve by doing so, etc.

To do this, you can utilize the exercise in the last chapter: <u>An Exercise For Identifying Limiting Beliefs</u>.

Let's start by learning a little bit more about your limiting belief. We want to really get in touch with it: what it feels like, what it looks like, what it does to you, etc.

Explore it fully. The sensation, the pain associated with it, and the limitations it has caused you.

If your limiting belief could talk, what would it say? Can you hear its voice? What does it sound like?

Maybe it sounds <u>just like you</u>. This is where I urge you to step outside of your box. Know that any voice that's bringing you down cannot possibly be your own.

Invite your belief to speak freely. Take the time to truly listen to this belief and everything it has to tell you. Don't argue with the belief; just let it say its part.

If it wants to tell you that you're no good, then let it tell you that you're no good. Let it assault you with everything it's got. Stay strong here: this is where many people will give up.

When it's finished saying what it needs to say, ask it why it said all of those things. Ask that voice in your head what the purpose of saying those things was.

When it responds, ask "Why?". Then listen to the response.

Again, ask "Why?". Then listen closely.

Keep asking and listening until you reach a stopping point where there are no more responses or the responses become weaker and weaker until they practically make no sense.

Your goal is either to expose the false logic of your limiting belief or to delve deeper into its choke hold on your life.

Thank your limiting belief for the responses. Thank it for its presence.

You may sit quietly for some time in gratitude at the opportunity to heal the limiting belief and improve your life.

Remember that the limiting belief wants a better life too. Instead of threatening to "remove" the belief, why not encourage it to join forces with you.

Suggest to the limiting belief that it would rather be at peace than at odds with you.

Tell it to trust you as you offer it a new way of thinking.

Take some of the things that your limiting belief wants to tell you, and recite them aloud. Tell yourself that you choose not to believe these things anymore. One-by-one, recite aloud the **opposite** of what the limiting belief wants to tell you.

Tell your limiting belief that you're making a choice to heal yourself. Assure the belief that this is also what it wants as well.

Guide your limiting belief into further expression of itself. Tell it that you Love it and that you want to listen to it.

If this belief made a sound, what would it be?

Go on. Make that sound aloud. Do it as many times as you wish until you feel like you fully understand it.

Then, make the opposite sound. What would the opposite of that feeling sound like? Continue to make that sound until you feel satisfied.

What facial expressions does the limiting belief make? Make those facial expressions until you're content. While doing this, just know that this is what you no longer wish to hang onto.

"Erase your face" from that expression by wiping/rubbing it off with your hands. Relax your face.

Now, what is the opposite of those facial expressions you just made? As best as you can, make the facial expressions that are the opposite of your limiting belief's.

In your mind, assert that these are the new facial expressions you wish to adopt. Wear them proudly. Notice how much better this feels.

Your limiting belief is subsiding. But continue to hear it through to the end.

Go on now and act out the limiting belief. What actions would it do if it were its own person? How would your limiting belief hold its body?

To the best of your ability, do a full-on impression of your limiting belief. Stand like it would stand. Walk like it would walk. Perform the actions that your limiting belief would perform.

Do this for as long as you wish or until it feels completely silly and/or unnatural. You may at this point feel a dramatic decline in the power that this belief ever had over you.

When you're finished with that, do what feels right in terms of erasing this impression from your muscle memory.

Feel free to shake, wiggle, scream, yell, grunt, moan, or roll around all over the floor for as long as you want. Don't give up! You're almost there!

Get that belief out of you. Spin, flail, move your body...do whatever you gotta do to engage your full self in emptying this belief from your cellular memory.

Once you're finished with that, take a few moments to recover and catch your breath.

Then, ask yourself what the opposite of that belief acts like. Stand as if you embodied the complete opposite of that belief.

Notice how your posture feels.

If you can, stand in front of the mirror as you're acting out your new belief. Observe your entire body: how it looks, how it feels.

Start from your head and work all the way down your body, acting out and feeling what it's like to have adopted the complete opposite of your limiting belief.

Do this for as long as feels comfortable.

Then just relax for a few moments in gratitude. Thank yourself. Thank God.

Once you've finished this, take a few long, slow, clean, crisp, refreshing breaths of air. You've done it. Be proud.

Now, go about the rest of your day, comrade.

Forget you even had this session and bear no expectations.

For now, just feel...

...just <u>be</u>.

Conclusion

I first want to say thank you for taking on the task of healing yourself and your limiting beliefs.

It takes a special kind of person to be willing to do this.

My hope is that you continue to delve deep inside yourself with the mission of making your life, and **the world**, a better place.

Remember to stay loving and light-hearted, as this is just the first day of the rest of your life.

You're going to encounter more limitations in the future, so brace yourself...

...and know that with each challenge awaits a new opportunity to blossom into a better version of you.

It's true: the world has poisoned you with negative beliefs. But before you start to blame, realize that **only you** could have allowed it to happen.

Also, bear in mind that this world is largely unconscious of its actions. Most people have no idea the extent of their harmful behavior. They, too, are subject to the powerful influence of limiting beliefs.

So when the world is trying to bring you down, just send it Love. Remember that no one or nothing can hurt you but yourself.

You are Spirit, whole and complete. The world can never take that away from you!

Note: I will talk more about freeing yourself from the world's influences in my next book, _The Gift: How To Rock The World, Wear Many Hats, And Still Be YOU In 2014_. I expect it to be done by December 15. If you want a free copy of it when it's complete, then please join my mailing list at align-mentality.com. As a bonus, I'll also send you the revolutionary, all-acclaimed Ascension Cheat Sheet. For free. Hell yeah!

The most crucial message that I want to deliver is that limiting beliefs can be so ingrained that they actually **feel** real.

It's remarkable the extent that people let their limiting beliefs dominate them.

For instance, I know someone who was incredibly thankful for the advice I gave them about limiting beliefs:

"Thanks, D/C, I now see how my beliefs about time were holding me back! I'd like to schedule a session with you, but as we all know reality sets in. So the next time I'm not busy I'll be in touch!"

Huh? What reality? There IS no reality.

I'm willing to bet that this person has way more time than she claims she does. She's harboring a belief that she's _too busy_ to pursue healing on the belief that's keeping her "_too busy_".

Because I guarantee that she's doing a lot of unnecessary things in her life to make her feel busy when she's actually not. I'm sure that a vast portion of her time is unnecessarily slipping away from her without her even knowing it.

I always keep this old Zen saying close to my heart because I think it's a powerful illustration of the seemingly contradictory nature of the universe: "You should sit in meditation for 20 minutes a day. But if you're too busy that day, then you should sit in meditation for an hour."

Oh, and check this out: It may be that she is, in fact, ridiculously busy and when she actually does have free time, she wants to spend it resting.

I can't blame her. But what if her limiting belief is manifesting in such a way that it's causing her to engage with life in a stressful manner. What if, for example, this person is actually doing/thinking/feeling something that unnecessarily drains her energy?

Did you know that negative emotions have a huge detriment on your energy levels? If you're holding onto anger against someone/something, you're the one who's getting burned.

I say all this to stress just how sneaky and how powerful limiting beliefs can be. They literally control each and every one of us in one way or another.

So keep your eyes open, comrade.

You know you're being utterly brainwashed by limiting beliefs when you have a tendency to point to some definition of 'reality'.

I read an internet post by a man infuriated by a Law of Attraction blog entry because he thought it was idealistic nonsense.

"That's great that you have time to pursue your dreams and everything is all hunky dory…but let's face it: some of us have things like obligations, mortgages, debt, and kids to raise. Not everyone can just be free to do whatever they please whenever their little hearts desire it. As good as all of this sounds, sometimes the best medicine is just to be realistic."

Man, talk about layers and layers of limiting beliefs...

With that being said, here's what I believe (and you can take it or leave it):

1) No matter who you are, where you are, what you're doing (or not doing), or what your present circumstances are, God can fix everything for you if you have faith in Him.

2) God **wants** you to be happy, abundant, Loving, and fulfilled.

3) The only force responsible for preventing you from having what you want is YOU and your limiting beliefs!

Well, that's all I got for now. Thank you for sharing this time with me, and I look forward to when we meet again!

Cheers.

Review Request

I wanted to make sure you got loads of value from this book. I truly hope it helps you to start making drastic changes in your life.

Please take a moment to write me a brief review on Amazon.

Reviews are extremely helpful for me. They also help me to reach a wider audience with this message.

You can leave a review by visiting this page:
http://amazon.com/dp/b00grelz3y

Thanks!

Bonus Power-Ups

Use these power-ups in combination with the jab methods to greatly enhance their efficacy.

Mantras

1) *"I am Spirit, whole and complete, all is Forgiven and released."*

2) *"I am ___."* Or, simply: *"I am."*

3) *"Even though I'm [insert emotion or limiting belief], I fully and deeply accept myself."*

Breathing Exercises

1) Diaphragmatic breathing is a technique that will help give you vitality and courage. It's where you use your diaphragm to create a vacuum that sucks air into your lungs. The way you do it is by pulling breath into your lungs by pushing out your belly as though you're trying to look pregnant. Don't pull with your chest, when you round out your belly, air will naturally fill your lungs. This is good because it gets air all the way to the bottom of your lungs, rather than just the top half during normal lung exhalation. It will help you pull energy all the way into your body and strengthen you as you perform emotional release.

2) Rapid breath is a technique that will energize your body. First start with completely empty lungs and then take rapid breaths where you inhale quickly and then exhale half of that amount. It's a "two steps forward, one step backward" approach to inhalation. If you do this rapidly, it will stimulate you and increase your energy.

3) Slow-nose breathing is a relaxation technique. First use your fingers to stretch and pull the skin on either side of your nose. Then inhale very slowly and steadily anywhere from 4-8 seconds. Hold at the top for 3-5 seconds. Then slowly and steadily exhale for 4-8 seconds.

Movements

Also as a power-up, consider doing things with your body. These can be simple stretches where you raise your arms up and slowly pull them back as far as they can go, pushing your chest outward. This will open up your heart chakra, allowing your emotions to flow more freely.

Another thing you can do is something active. I recommend throwing assorted punches in the air or doing jumping jacks. The reasoning behind this is that it will get you blood pumping, thus stimulating energy flow throughout your body. I like to stare at myself in a full-length mirror while doing something energetic. At the same time, I'm telling myself positive affirmations that build my confidence and rewire my belief system.

And, of course, yoga is a great way to cleanse the mind and the heart through the body. You don't have to be a master yogi to immediately begin to feel the hugely beneficial effects.

Meditation Power-Up

A final way to connect with your limiting beliefs even deeper is through meditation. You can use the process I laid out in order to identify the limiting belief and then sit still while you contemplate the limiting belief.

Feel free to visualize the belief melting away, your neuropathways rerouting, or anything else that helps you to connect with the process of rewiring your limiting belief.

You can use any or all of the jab methods while you're sitting still, allowing yourself to become one with the limiting belief. Don't try to force anything. Just sit still and simply allow yourself to be. Accept yourself as you are and breathe calmly and relaxed.

You'll notice anywhere from 100 to 300 million thoughts fly through your head, making it incredibly difficult to focus. That's OK. Just let your brain do its thing and don't try to change anything. Just sit still and chill out.

Identity Shifting

Right as I was about to publish this book, I ran across an extremely illuminating article that describes how you can overcome limiting beliefs by taking on another identity.
http://goodvibeblog.com/manifesting-with-identity-shifting/

When I read it, I just HAD to share it as a power-up. I hope this additional resource also helps you!

Closing Remarks

Again, thanks for reading *Manifest NOW*. May all of your decisions come from a place of strength and positive intention.

Remember that your limiting beliefs are always in effect. Even the tiniest bit of detective work will reveal them to you. When you have a negative emotional reaction to something, there is certainly a limiting belief behind it. If you ever find yourself pointing to some "fixed" version of reality, you can bet your bottom dollar that you're being run by a limiting belief.

A limiting belief is something you believe that limits you. It's only a belief...**not** reality. And make no mistake, limiting beliefs are everywhere. Just keep making a small effort every day to chip away at them and over time your life will be completely different.

Keep in mind that no one is going to do this work for you. And if you don't do it now, it's likely that you never will. You will die never having achieved your dreams.

I wish you the best of luck on your journey, comrade. And I invite you to keep in touch via email by signing up to my website: hand-coded and every stitch placed there by Yours Truly. I designed every page, every entry, with *you* in mind. Take a look, let me know if you like it: Align-Mentality.com.

But before you do anything else, take a moment to write a review for this book. It'll help me out a lot.

Until next time...

Signed,

D/C Russ

be bold. stay strong.

Alignmentality - The place where we know no limitations.

More Books by D/C

STOP!! Manifesting Money: Stunning Law of Attraction Advice You've NEVER Heard About
http://amazon.com/dp/b00ewok94m
STOP!! Manifesting Money suggests that in order to truly attract abundance you have to be clear on exactly what you want (not "money"). Then, you must **align yourself** with it. This book will give you straightforward insight on precisely how to do this.

Manifestation Resistance: The #1 Reason Why You Are Unsuccessful with The Law of Attraction
http://amazon.com/dp/b00d69qtg6
Manifestation Resistance is a book that talks about the common ways people prevent themselves from reaching their goals and dreams in life. It also proposes simple solutions that you can use in order to start achieving what you want.

When Wisdom Whispers: The Art of Following Your Heart to a Life You Love
http://www.amazon.com/dp/B00HH5PFWE
These days it seems like our paths are carved out for us: do good in school, go to a good college, get a good job, save for retirement, and then die. But somewhere along the lines we forgot about the Love and Passion that following your heart can bring. This book will teach you *exactly* how to follow your own inner wisdom and pursue a life of Happiness, Freedom, and Abundance.

Lessons from the Universe: 365 Daily Entries Along My Journey to Faith, Freedom, and Prosperity
http://www.amazon.com/dp/B00IN136JU
Every day for an entire year, I wrote exactly 101 words about the most profound experience from that day. The lessons in this book are timeless and they will undoubtedly resonate with you on a very deep level. Topics include love, success, dreams, goals, persistence, emotions, pain & struggle, faith, failure, endurance, surrender, time, humanity, freedom, and magic powers.

The Gift: 5 Little Abundance Secrets You Forgot You Knew
http://www.amazon.com/dp/B00HAX44UW
If you are a person and you have a heartbeat, then you also have the ability to gain the success, love, and happiness that you desire. The Gift will help you unlock your potential by reminding you why abundance is your birthright. It is a short book that inspires gratitude for the gifts we all possess.

I WOULD RATHER DIE!!: Fight Your Financial Failure with Ferocity
http://www.amazon.com/dp/B00JFFYVB0
If you're fed up with not having the abundance you want, this book is for you. If being weighed down by your finances has finally gotten on your last nerve, this book is for you. And if you're ready to break free from stressing out about money, then this book is definitely for you.

Quest for Smiles: 15 Mini-Missions to Cheer You Up and Brighten Your Day
http://amazon.com/dp/B00JKB08HK

It's too easy these days to be so busy that you forget to look out for your own happiness. This book offers 15 very simple activities you can do by yourself or with a friend. These activities are designed with one goal in mind: to help you be happier. This book is short and highly readable and is sure to uplift and refresh you.

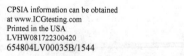

CPSIA information can be obtained
at www.ICGtesting.com
Printed in the USA
LVHW081722300420
654804LV00035B/1544